DEC   2016

TENNIS

BY KARA L. LAUGHLIN

Published by The Child's World®
1980 Lookout Drive • Mankato, MN 56003-1705
800-599-READ • www.childsworld.com

ACKNOWLEDGMENTS
The Child's World®: Mary Swensen, Publishing Director
The Design Lab: Design
Heidi Hogg: Editing
Sarah M. Miller: Editing

PHOTO CREDITS
© David Lee/Shutterstock.com: 2-3; ER_09/Shutterstock.com: 4;
Goran Bogicevic/Shutterstock.com: 9; g-stockstudio/Shutterstock.
com: 14-15; Kaspars Grinvalds/Shutterstock.com: cover, 1;
Lance Bellers/Shutterstock.com: 16; lev radin/Shutterstock.
com: 7; LouLouPhotos/Shutterstock.com: 19; wavebreakmedia/
Shutterstock.com: 13; Zorandim/Shutterstock.com: 10; zulufoto/
Shutterstock.com: 20-21

ISBN: 9781503807822
LCCN: 2015958126

Printed in the United States of America
Mankato, MN
June, 2016
PA02300

TABLE OF CONTENTS

4

Time to Play!

The sun is warm. The air is calm. It is a great day for tennis!

You will need balls and a **racket**. You also need a court to play on. Tennis courts are hard and flat. A **net** splits the court into two sides.

Fast Fact!

Wearing good tennis shoes is important! You must be able to run and change directions quickly.

Who Can Play?

Two or four people can play. For **singles**, one person plays on each side. In **doubles**, there are two players per team.

7

Starting the Game

The **server** starts the game. She throws the ball in the air. She hits it with her racket. Whoosh! It whizzes across the court.

Fast Fact!
The fastest serve ever recorded happened in 2012.
The ball flew at 163.4 miles (almost 263 kilometers) per hour!

9

Faults

The ball might land in the wrong spot. If so, it is a **fault**. The server tries again. Two faults in a row make a **double fault**. Then the other side wins a point.

The same player serves again. The ball sails over the net! Now the other player must return the serve.

Fast Fact!
Tennis became an Olympic sport in 1896. It was removed from the official list in 1924. It was brought back in 1988.

Rallying

Players **rally** until one player makes an error. Maybe he hits the ball into the net. Maybe he can't hit it back at all. He might hit the ball **out of bounds**. Then the other team scores a point.

Fast Fact!
Tennis balls are made of rubber and a fabric called felt.

GAMES

POINTS

3

30

2

40

16

Points

Tennis points have special names. Instead of 0, 1, 2, 3, and 4, they are called **love**, 15, 30, 40, and **game**. A player wins when they reach game (4 points).

Fast Fact!
At pro tennis events, an umpire sits in a tall chair.
Judges on the court watch the ball and players.
The umpire and judges make sure everything is fair.

In tennis, there are games, **sets**, and **matches**. The goal is to win the match. Six games can win a set. Two sets can win a match.

Fast Fact!
The longest match ever recorded happened in London in 2010. It lasted 11 hours and 5 minutes!

0 SETS WON 0 SETS WON 1 5

When the match is over, the players go to the net. They shake hands. It was a good game!

Glossary

double fault (DUB-bul FAWLT): A double fault is a second bad serve in a row.

doubles (DUB-buls): A doubles tennis game has two people on each side.

fault (FAWLT): A bad serve. The server gets to try again.

game (GAYM): The fourth and final point in tennis is called game.

love (LUV): The word for zero in tennis scores is love.

matches (MATCH-ez): Matches are groups of at least two sets won by a player.

net (NET): Open fabric stretched across the tennis court. The ball must go over the net.

out of bounds (OWT of BOWNDZ): A ball hit outside of the boundary lines on a tennis court is out of bounds.

racket (RAK-et): A paddle-shaped piece of tennis gear strung with a grid of cord. The grid gives the ball extra bounce.

rally (RAL-lee): A series of hits across the net. A rally begins with a serve and ends when a player scores.

server (SURV-er): The player who hits the ball at the beginning of each rally. Servers serve a full game and rotate through a match.

sets (SETS): Sets are groups of at least six games won by a player.

singles (SING-ulz): A singles tennis game has one person on each side.

To Learn More

In the Library

Gifford, Clive. *Tennis*. London: Franklin Watts, 2015.

Morey, Allan. *Tennis*. Minneapolis, MN:
Bullfrog Books/Jump!, 2015.

Rausch, David. *United States Tennis Association*.
Minneapolis, MN: Bellwether Media, 2015.

On the Web

Visit our Web site for links about tennis:
childsworld.com/links

Note to Parents, Teachers, and Librarians: We routinely verify
our Web links to make sure they are safe and active sites.
So encourage your readers to check them out!

Index

About the Author

Kara L. Laughlin is an artist and writer who lives in Virginia with her husband, three kids, two guinea pigs, and a dog. She is the author of two dozen nonfiction books for kids.